SKULLS AND HIBISCUS

SKULLS AND HIBISCUS

HEATHER VAZQUEZ

NEW DEGREE PRESS

COPYRIGHT © 2021 HEATHER VAZQUEZ

All rights reserved.

SKULLS AND HIBISCUS

ISBN	978-1-63676-932-5	*Paperback*
	978-1-63676-996-7	*Kindle Ebook*
	978-1-63730-100-5	*Ebook*

these poems are dedicated to:

people who spend nights overthinking life, social media junkies, anime nerds, friends, and the relatives who thought I was going to slip up because they didn't like my mom

CONTENTS

HONEY	11
PROPOSAL	12
ALL-NIGHTERS	13
CONFESSION	14
RUBIES	15
DEVOTION IN ONESELF	16
NIGHTCRAWLER	17
LOVE LESSONS	18
YOUR PERSON	19
COMFORT	20
ケージド	21
PILLOWTALKING TO MYSELF	22
GUARDED	23
SECRETS	24
ALONE	25
TOGETHER	26
UNFORTUNATE	27
A BIG HEART	28
WORTH	29
REMEMBER TO TAKE CARE OF YOURSELF	30
SHORT-LIVED	31
SECOND STAR TO THE RIGHT	32
ANONYMOUS	34
GROW UP	35
HUMAN	36

PARENTS	37
NUMB	38
PATERNAL CHAOS	39
SELF-AWARE	40
HOME	41
TAKE A BREAK	43
TOO POLITE	44
FRIENDS	45
POP CULTURE ESCAPISM	46
STRESS	47
ADULT	48
WITHIN	49
INVINCIBLE	50
FALLING OUT	51
FORGET ME NOT	52
AHEAD	53
A BAD WEEK	54
CIRCUS	56
TICKING	57
PLASTIC	59
TITLE IX	60
WIRES	61
OVERTHINKING ME	62
MANLY	63
NOW IT'S SUNDAY	65
MELODY	67
OPTIONS	68
IT COULD BE WORSE	69
NOTHING LASTS FOREVER	70
BEYOND 9–5	71

CONTENT WITH MISERY	72
WICKED	73
LOSS	74
TIME DOESN'T HEAL EVERYTHING	75
YES OR NO?	76
FRAGILE	78
EMOTIONS	79
EXPIRING	80
MORE THAN FRIENDS	81
OBLIVION	82
PLATONIC	83
I'M FINE	84
OUTCAST	85
GRUDGES	86
FOR VICTORIA	87
THINGS LEFT UNSAID	88
YOU	89
GUM	90
NICE GUYS	91
CORONATION	92
DARK ROAST	93
SEESAW OF THE MIND	94
CHEATER	95
USEFUL	96
REPEAT AFTER ME	97
FLY	98
THOUGHTS	99
IF I HAD WINGS	100
PERCEPTION	101
YOU WERE CALLED COURAGE	102

CHAPTERS	103
REDISCOVERY	104
LOVESICK	105
DEAD POETS SOCIETY	106
WHALEN 52	107
ACKNOWLEDGEMENTS	109
APPENDIX	111

Honey

Over tea

I want to tell my grandma, life can be really shitty,

like

really shitty,

you have to go to school in order to be

what society deems "successful,"

then work, work harder in order to make money

because that's just how the world functions.

Painfully bitter
the wholesomeness carried by her yesteryears is no more.

Children don't blossom the same,

hearts do not ache the same,

grins don't widen the same,

it's a shame.

No matter how much honey she puts in my tea,
It'll never be as sweet as hers.

Proposal

Don't offer me the love of a butterfly: some only last a day.

If you're not cautious enough it'll die,
withering away like some of
the hearts that walk this Earth.

Instead, aim for a love as grand as a tree with branches strong, hugging the sky, blooming endlessly.

A love that can outlive all for centuries.

All-Nighters

We were only going to talk for a few minutes,

maybe an hour.

but then we started to laugh and make games,

talking about recent scars, past pains

before we knew it, the sun rose.

I didn't want to sleep,

didn't feel tired,

wanted to know the sky you slept under

whether it was the same as mine.

Confession

I hadn't carried an idea of what a perfect person was and honestly it didn't settle in until this year until I finally thought about what I wanted in a partner. I like the idea of building a foundation with someone emotionally, always progressing to do better. I want you to call me out on my bullshit or irrationality 'cause I can be a handful at times.

I'm not settling for less, and I know you're not either, as we've been able to support each other throughout our time knowing one another. There will be moments where we behave annoyingly and fight over the little things. Truthfully, I'm pretty excited to do that with you 'cause at the end of the day we've got the desire to work together as a team.

You're not perfect, and there are sides I haven't seen. You hold flaws you prefer to keep hidden, and though you may not believe it, I find you perfect for me. I understand relationships don't just require happiness but compromise and you're the person I want to do all that with.

All I truly want is you.

Rubies

She may be a diamond
but within my eyes, you're a ruby.
A gem all the same,
both crafted from nature's soil.
She represents light,
you're a flame
in its purest form.
She reflects the winds
that change the seasons,
and you are the sun
that gives life to the Earth.
She's the purest joys,
you're the most courageous
of passions.
You are a ruby,
one with flushed cheeks
gold in your eyes,
she is a diamond
with soft smiles
a gaze mimicking,
the morning skies.
So yes, she may be a diamond
but you are a ruby within my eyes.

Devotion in Oneself

Take in the air around you,
exhale the night,
be mindful
there's certainty
in becoming uncertain
about your path

The freckles and scarring
that adorn your face
serve as a reminder of the trials
achieved,
those yet to be finished

So, when you look upon the moon,
remember
there are marigolds
blooming beneath
the soles of your feet

You're a boundless entity:
acknowledge yourself

Nightcrawler

Tonight, I met a man who looked like the moon,

starlight hair, sapphire eyes

strumming his black guitar,

singing of some place a bit too far.

He spoke like an old ghost that wanders around

through empty streets in this small town.

Each freckle on his face, a granted token

of countless hurt left unspoken,

as soon as his first tear shed

I wanted to live inside his head.

His heart was a labyrinth of pain,

disguised by playful games.

Scars guard his soul in a bind,

damaging him whenever he's kind.

If I'm able to open his eyes,

he'll realize his stars are held in the skies.

Love Lessons

It really pisses me off when someone says, "I'll love you unconditionally." Unconditionally means no restrictions, no consequences. This implies there's room to cheat, lie, manipulate, or leave you six feet under. Love is not meant to cause pain, but rather heal in order to obtain its highest level of growth. No one can teach you to love properly, yet it still holds boundaries. These boundaries lead to a love you fully deserve.

Stop settling for something less than you are and find a love that challenges and inspires you. Find a love that makes you wonder about the world and its inhabitants. Let it soar so you may finally touch the sky and guide you to infinite abundance.

Love conditionally.

Your Person

There will come a time

when someone will devote themselves

to caring for you,

not considering you a burden,

showering you

with a form of affection

previously unacquired,

a person who gives

as much as they take

reassuring your heart,

never filling you with uncertainty

on the future.

Comfort

It's hard to believe a simple expression can enchant the way I view my world. Yet here I stand, the walls of my despair now crumbled to ash beneath my feet. A simple grin, laced with love placed in front of me, reminding me of who I am, what I can, and cannot change. Though the moment is bittersweet, it fills me with hope for tomorrows, the next weeks, or next years. I have reassurance that the sun that kisses my flesh will still remain warm even on the coldest of days.

ケージド

(Caged)

I'm caged in the love you gave me,

love that filled me with bliss,

that destroyed every fiber of me,

picking off piece by piece,

until there was but a seed

left of my sanity.

The flower may have gone,

but my roots still remain ready

to be reborn while yours have dried.

I feel relieved;

you no longer rule my garden.

安心しました

あなたはもう私の庭を支配していません

Pillowtalking to Myself

You lie next to me without a sound and I can't help but overthink if you truly love me. Not like, 'Oh I love you, you're my one and only,' like you feel you'll die tomorrow if you can't see my face. Would your heart stop beating if I leave or will it crack? You've seen my skin, but do you see my bruises and scars? Do you know what I dream about, what frightens me? Do you know what excites me and what makes me cry? Do you accept me for who I am, or do you want me to change? Do you feel what I feel when I look into your eyes?

I'll ask you: do you love me?

Guarded

Sometimes love harbors more pain

than bargained for.

You can't allow anyone

to love you because there's so much love

you lack in yourself.

Still, there's that longing for affection,

and adoration,

as you develop the need to feel whole.

Secrets

Imagine

you give your heart

to another,

in hopes they cherish it

like their own;

you entrust them

with words and thoughts

you'd never dare say

out loud, once more.

Your aspirations and past,

all these aspects

that hold pride or shame,

making who you are.

Only for them

to tell the world,

when they leave,

chilling, isn't it?

Alone

It's troubling

when you're the one holding the umbrella

for others during the storm,

then, once caught in the rain,

greeted with black clouds,

soaked in your thoughts.

Together

We're trying to love ourselves on a planet that shows us we're much smaller than we think we are. It's a hard path to walk, but I'm holding your hand, knowing we have a chance to be significant. So, let us believe in each other so that you can see yourself the way that I have always seen you.

Unfortunate

I wish I looked like the pretty girls my peers described,

the ones with the light eyes and beauty inscribed.

I wish I dressed like a porcelain toy

since pretty boys nowadays like girls with poise.

They love a soft voice

small waist

no choice

encased,

the ones that will follow all the rules,

that society's man will tell them to do,

a part of me wishes I did have this all,

trading this freedom would be my greatest downfall.

A Big Heart

I care way too much for others,
and it's unbearable
to give more of this light of mine
while they take everything,
and in the end
they never really care;
I only remain a star in their eyes
when they want me
to be seen,
a mere memory within the sky.

Worth

Be with the person

who gives you their best

without being asked,

going the extra mile

to take you on an adventure.

They'll remember your favorite drink,

the song that makes you smile,

how to ease you

when the sky is crashing down.

They'll add more color to your world,

shining brighter than the sun,

illuminating your nights.

Though it feels

that this person may not exist,

that these fragments are embedded

only in storybooks,

they're more real

than you believe.

Remember to Take Care of Yourself

Be the guardian

you always needed

when you were younger,

allowing yourself to grieve,

to be angry,

knowing it's okay

that giving your best

may not be enough.

Short-Lived

Life is temporary; as chilling as it may seem, it's brilliant. Like the seasons, our souls come and go, allowing us to grow far greater than we may ever understand. Death shouldn't put you in fear as there are wondrous aspects that lead to it. Our hair starts to mimic the clouds in the sky as the sun continues to grace the patterns on our skin, knowledge expanding, and though our vision may leave us, there are memories to be gained. We learn to laugh more like children and love as if it were endless, becoming soldiers of this Earth, our hearts held high as shields. We are given the chance to live radiantly.

Second Star to the Right

A fallen star yet to be discovered by others,

giving me the honor of knowing your name.

It's two in the morning and I can't help but wonder

if you and I are actually the same,

mirroring one another under this blackened sky.

Yet, you don't quite see yourself clearly as I do.

Your energy exudes a yellow hue,

a grand fire with a gentle flame.

A lost boy is what you are,

allow me to be lost with you,

so that I

may be the sky that holds up all your stars.

Confide in me so the scars crossed on your heart heal,

so that your demons may be put to rest,

and may the shadows break, making way for new light.

Let that radiance guide you to a pure love,

one that knows both friend and foe,

a love that carries compassion and truth.

Once that's revealed,

you will see that you're the star shining brightest in the night.

Peter Pan, directed by Clyde Geronimi (1953; Burbank: Walt Disney Productions, 1990), film.

Anonymous

I don't know you,
but I know you're enough.

I may not know your story,
nor how it may end,
but you're worth reading.

Don't let anyone
take that away from you.

Grow Up

Yes, but don't rush
there's still so much more
left for you to do.
You'll find new people
to laugh with,
more hands to hold,
changes you can't help
but adapt to.
The journey that lies ahead of you
is terrifying,
but it's yours:
go at your own pace.

Human

I like to believe people are good at heart,

but it becomes harder as each day passes.

Humans *can* be selfish.

They can hurt, steal, cheat, lie,

some don't suffer consequences

I try my best to understand others,

but I can't understand *those* people

how they can be so horrible,

how did we get to this point

where we refused to act humane

towards each other?

Parents

I've tried my best to satisfy their needs because I had craved so desperately for the phrase "we're proud" but I don't fully believe I'll ever be enough nor that I deserve even an ounce of praise and I want to trust that I am able to serve others while aiding myself but that moment feels centuries away from where I stand

Numb

I'm walking in circles, my days the same with nothing changed. Life is gray and it's frustrating that I have yet to find my own colors in this world, my own passions, and desires. A figure of flesh and blood stomping constantly upon the concrete, holding no real purpose. And though I'm still young, I've already met the end of a road.

So, I guess I'll just create my own.

Paternal Chaos

I was not upset over the things you did,

I'm furious that you act as if they didn't happen

like you were picture perfect.

I remember the yelling,

I remember the glares,

I remember getting compared to everyone

except myself.

I reminisce the moments that I felt young

when I didn't know any better,

thought fondly of you,

I barely talk to you,

as I can't,

you state it's possible

but no amount of paint

can cover the canvas of scars you left on me.

Self-Aware

It pains me to realize
that those around me,
seek light in me,
find me worthy of
so much promise,
offering blessings and grace,
while I deem myself
as useless as my own shadow.

Though I know
I hold purpose,
there's a darkness that swallows me,
forcing me to believe
life and I
were never meant to be.

Home

¿Por qué estás ansioso?

You have no reason to be anxious.

Why are you upset?

There's a roof above your head,

the things my mother would say to me.

A competition of who felt worse,

who worked longer, who tried harder,

nobody ever won

Sitting across the table are pride and misery

as I replay each mistake made,

each error that could've been prevented,

only to bang my head against the wall

Because, again, *I* have no reason to be anxious

¿Hay una razón?

Growing up too quickly, worrying about each day

working tirelessly with no help

opening your heart for people who should never stay,

and the picture's too clear

as the toxicity of the atmosphere

wraps his hands around my neck

all I can scream,

"powerless"

Take a Break

It hurts to no longer want to be responsible. Your body feels burnt out, howling for you to stop. Sadly, you refuse, because you believe that if you do, everything you've worked for will fall apart

Too Polite

Hello.

Sorry to be a bother,

I don't want to impose

but if you could excuse my actions

I would highly appreciate it.

My mother said

I'm far too nice

for others and

for my own good,

stating both "please" and "thank you"

at least twice a day,

even if it were

to throw my feelings away.

Friends

No one ever told me that having friends would be so lonely. We could rummage through malls, play games, and hear music, but it's all so detached. I am in a theatre, alone, watching them upon the screen.

Pop Culture Escapism

Tutorials, downloads, comments, likes—

her web has restrained me of my being.

My attention stuck to a screen mindlessly,

allowing anime or music to drown my room,

the TV is screaming,

my ears are ringing,

people keep asking me to go out

but I'm *far* too busy

with her barricading my door,

it's not that easy,

each day that passes feels like an eternity

so she greets me and weaves me

into this abyss threaded with false realities

and ignorant bliss.

Stress

The clock moves fast, yet not fast enough;

you carry too many tasks and no motivation,

knowing what needs to be done.

Incredibly prideful,

no need to ask for help,

helping others because that's what you do best,

becoming the matchmaker,

peacemaker,

caretaker,

what would happen if the clock stopped?

Adult

It sucks having to be the bigger person. You want to be childish, a bit more selfish without worrying about any consequences at hand. Take a step and be wiser than you already are. This moment will be much more rewarding in the future, guiding you toward a path of fulfillment, allowing you to succeed what may be deemed as impossible.

Within

Look into my eyes and you'll see,

a once happy child caged by insecurity.

All grown up, yet still restricted

by those who test her limits;

a procrastinating perfectionist

who makes the grade at the deadline

only to assign herself

more work so she feels enough,

to become useful and needed.

She starves more for success

than happiness,

the child forever a memory.

Look into my eyes, your reflection caught,

tell me what *you* see.

Invincible

I love seeing a child behave so freely. Still unsure about the world, as they fall in love with music or words they don't yet understand, with the idea that they can accomplish their goals no matter what life throws at them, they can fall, get hurt, but they continue to rise because they believe that everything is attainable.

Falling Out

To those whom I've let go in my life, please know it was my fault too. I carry no malice, rather I miss you and hope for the best. I pray you receive all you've been wanting and that this life brings more opportunities than expected. We had a journey that changed us both, and though we cared enough for one another, our connection was already broken before meeting its end.

Forget Me Not

Your laugh echoes in my room,

Old Spice and coffee filling the air.

I still remember the curls in your hair

like salt and pepper, always covered by a cap.

You used to sing to everyone in the house,

dancing around with no music playing,

your gold monogrammed necklace,

swinging along your shirt,

sound always following you.

I miss your cooking, stories of younger years.

Fireworks still light up the night on your birthday,

but it hasn't been the same since you passed away.

It still hurts to wander near your grave,

"Beloved" engraved below your name,

performing many roles

aiding those in life,

how you played grandpa in mine.

Ahead

I'm scared of growing into myself,

not because I fear my full potential,

rather knowing when I do,

I'll leave behind those

who refuse to better themselves.

A Bad Week

Eyes out of focus

this big lump in my throat,

a scream freeing itself

while I smother it with my teeth.

Trying my hardest to block it

I play music,

keep raising the volume

and no matter how much the bass bumps

my head pounds harder

a tortured melody of flat keys;

trying to stay in tune

to keep my heartbeat steady

and my hands from shaking,

the tears from bursting,

but I'm suffocating

you, who keeps sipping on cheap wine

as I whine over my worries.

I've become too weary,

too nauseous to eat,

but you would never know

Circus

When your head keeps spinning

it's difficult to stay at peace,

walking the wire to be a victim of society.

As a child you're taught right from wrong

not from your own free will

rather from the will of others, leading to conformity

you do your best to avoid mistakes

lest you plummet toward the bottom

making you an instrument for a stage called "Life".

Ticking

The clock keeps on while my eyes remain open,

hands sweating, heart pounding.

I can hear it in my ears,

ghost howling in my head,

but the clock keeps ticking.

It ticks and tocks above my head, reminding me of past regrets.

hell, it spins

around like a pinwheel powered by neurotics

my over obsessive tendencies rising to the surface

overthinking the little things becomes a bit too overwhelming

I'd like to state that I'm fine but really, I'm in a fight,

not with others but myself. I am my own worst enemy

I'm the ringleader and spectator of a deadly scenery.

I've orchestrated this torment within my head

because I feel alive, yet at the same time dead?

What I mean is

my body is here but my soul's numb

the clock keeps singing its stupid song.

It ticks and tocks and the spirit screams louder

At this point, I feel like I've lost my power

I'm tired of keeping myself under control.

I feel like a bird with no sense of direction

and I don't know where else to go.

Plastic

A film is cast over my eyes in the dark,

as a reminder to play my role.

I'm a doll, hanging from my family tree,

a black pawn among the king and queen,

held up by a string

my lips stay sealed within the night

because I can't answer

why my house shakes as if it'll break, or

why my water tastes like gin

and how it burns

a dry lie

made to paint a picture that no longer exists

a fantasy derived from smiles and laughter

coating screams and berry-colored skin.

Title IX

Somewhere on the street, makeup stains her face.

He walks her home to be safe,

but she can't report the marks on her legs

lest the school be marked a disgrace

It's her fault:

look at her clothes

It's her fault:

alcohol on her breath

It's her fault:

she didn't say no

but she didn't say yes.

Now that bastard walks free,

while her life's a wreck

Wires

It hurts to appear happy
when all you want to do
is just give up.
Not because you yearn to leave,
you're just tired.
Your body's here
but your mind remains
somewhere far
as it seems that
anything else would be better
than being inside your own skin.
No one would know
all the screams
you kept restrained by smiles.
No one sees
the chains around your neck
tucked under your jacket,
now you believe
that there's nothing left
to grab onto
as you're drained
from holding yourself together.
It feels like you're hanging on a wire,
waiting for it to snap
so you can finally fall.
You crave it so damn badly,
that you forget
those you'd leave behind.

Overthinking Me

There are days I love myself, grateful for the life I live. However, I carry days in which I wish I did not live at all, to be a figment of someone else's imagination. Thoughts like weights placed upon my ankles, each step heavier until I give up. It's hard to survive when your mind splits in two. Then everything becomes increasingly shittier. Nitpicking like I'm my worst enemy. I need to be smarter, work harder, but once these expectations are met, the trivial becomes my biggest problem. Eat less, exercise more, cut my hair, grow it out, remember to smile, never shout, be needed, be useful, lest I become my own nightmare.

Manly

Don't feel, just act cool

grit those teeth, get wild

dive into your alcohol,

and if life's too much to handle,

tough shit, don't ask for help

You'll have to solve it on your own.

Hit the gym, start bulking up

you have to look tough to be desirable

Fight with your friends

get destructive, there's no time for peace

Chase a woman 'til she says yes

then break her heart

so you don't seem weak.

Steer clear of anything

remotely feminine

or

No one will take you seriously

You're a human,

don't listen to this crap

they shouldn't define you

you're man enough to take on society.

Now It's Sunday

The mirror's become
my friendliest enemy
motivating Mondays,
tear-me-down Tuesdays,
wishing my skin
another's on Wednesdays.

Though Thursdays
allow me to be thankful,
that this temple
bestowed upon me
is my own,
each scar,
each freckle,
each hair,
which lays upon it
suspects this gift
is actually a curse.

I fear the Fridays
that force me to gaze at my thighs
as they expand my jeans
or shorten a black dress,
leaving a bitter taste
on my tongue.

That sourness lurks around Saturdays
and the looking glass calls me once more,
drowning my thoughts with questions,
toying with my figure like clay.

Is the texture of my skin changing?
Has my chest gotten smaller or am I just
getting bigger?
Why is my waist broad?
Why isn't it narrow?
Why can't my hair grow longer?
Why can't I be leaner?
Why can't I be pretty?
Why? Why? Why?

Now it's Sunday:
the cycle starts again.

Melody

If I were a song and you the singer,
how would I be sung?
Does my tune remain frail or
is it strong enough to get under your skin?
Am I so powerful I can make you smile,
or do I overwhelm you like a bad memory?

Options

No one enjoys being the second choice.

To be the 'other,'

not the 'one,'

makes me suppose

I wasn't good enough to be kept in your thoughts,

rather a repressed memory behind your mind

rewound to remind you

I could benefit you,

to wonder whether

I'm worthy

of ever being first.

It Could Be Worse

You're right

it can be worse,

but that doesn't excuse the agony.

You can be grateful for the life you have

and still suffer,

just as one smiles in the day

but weeps at night.

It's okay to break.

Unsatisfied?

Hell, you can be angry at life

because it's *yours*.

It's not pretty all the time,

it can be cruel, painful,

don't hide this frustration.

Embrace it.

Nothing Lasts Forever

Death is inevitable,

she's feared

bringing togetherness

heartache

creating division

releasing ignorance.

There's dread

within her power,

holding a beauty

unseen

truth behind

human nature,

pure fear. . .

Beyond 9–5

Typing, eating, working

have become simple means of routine

then coming home

cooking, cleaning, and drinking

have become luxuries less than a blessing.

The clock keeps ticking

and the leaves keep changing

but to simply exist has been much more taxing

than the tasks and demands

I'm meant to meet daily

because feeling alive has lost its meaning

forcing me to believe happiness can't pair with reality.

Content with Misery

One of the most painful requests I have ever received was to live my life as I pleased. It's not because I believe that goal is unattainable, rather it's been instilled within my head that this objective is not meant for people like me. Those who've learned to dance with their sadness. Why? Because if it was up to me, I would have just remained as roots underneath the soil. I wouldn't carry any suffering, any palms to ache, or hearts to break. To become a beautiful seed of the Earth sounds more purposeful as I can go about my pain in silence.

Wicked

Ever have those days when you hate humanity?

Not as a concept but because of their behavior,

people become so damn horrible

that it physically urges me to vomit.

We've become divided in this world,

"every man for himself"

a shield against common decency

until we're no longer human.

Loss

When you lose someone you've cherished,

be it through death or separation,

a part of you is lost and regained,

putting the malevolent demon

right there under the bed.

Though you sleep with lights on,

there's this darkness

that continues to rise,

assuring you

an unforeseen future.

Time Doesn't Heal Everything

Sometimes time drives people mad.

For some, grieving lasts a second

for others, a lifetime.

While we were together,

I missed who I was

when you left,

you took a part of me too.

I don't believe that

can be recovered.

Yes or No?

Hello, people pleaser.

You're a shadow in a story,

not even an antagonist

the middleman,

a mediator,

the person people depend on

who *can't* rely on others,

but needs the most help.

Why?

Because it takes less time

to smile with gritted teeth

than to say 'no'

and feel selfish.

So,

you comply without question,

no yes or no,

thrown to the ground

as a tacky doormat,

muddy footprints

piling one after the other,

you endure pressure

because losing yourself is better than

feeling like a failure to others.

Fragile

Your eyes are cracked

like broken glass

held within a picture frame.

Each repair made

pricked your skin,

shards missing in the end.

Memories sliced into your hands

yet a desire to heal remains

as you can't accept not fixing

what is already broken.

Emotions

Please remember

that it's okay to cry.

If all you know is silence,

let your tears

speak for you.

Silence can be painful

but when it comforts,

it can remind us

that we're not alone.

There's strength under your feet

even if you believe

the floor will crumble.

Expiring

You told me love sucks, I couldn't believe you,

rightfully, you hated the world

so, you thought there was no need to stay,

stay and live a life that gives you purpose,

in feeling fulfilled with friends,

who'd never call or share,

their feelings, hoping to reciprocate.

Love sucks, though, and I believed you,

you taught me a new perspective only to leave,

leave me in a black dress, heart torn in two.

Two hearts meant to beat as one and yours stopped.

More Than Friends

I can't pretend it doesn't hurt
when your eyes wander someone else's way,
I wish you roamed mine.
To be in love seemed a myth—
still, you're here beside me
singing that song,
the one that heightens your heartache
while bringing me pain,
your heart entwined with your voice,
hoping that maybe
perhaps,
I could heal what's broken.

Oblivion

I keep talking to the moon,

only to be met with silence.

She twinkles mockingly,

lowering down

and the day begins anew

leaving me alone in my room.

Light piercing through the shades,

yearning for darkness

to revive last night once more.

So, what do I do?

I told her my secrets,

and it appears she left me, too.

Platonic

I love you but not in that way. I respect you for all you've accomplished. You've made me better, helped me to grow. You carry every reason to be angry with the world, yet you still choose to smile and welcome it with open arms. I don't think I could ever succeed in that, but the thought brings me comfort, to believe there are still good things in life. That's why walking beside rather than behind you is a challenge. Although we are both growing at our own pace, you're already way ahead of me.

I'm Fine

I'm not,
and I'm not sure
I will ever fully feel
'Fine.'

To shout that everything is wrong
until my lungs give out
because I've hidden myself
for so long.

I want to experience emotion
and know for once
I will ever truly be
'Okay.'

Outcast

I'm lost, misplaced as though I don't fully belong to this world. I'm taking up space among a society that isn't even my own, gradually losing what is left of my being. I haven't lived my life seriously enough to feel alive, merely surviving, depicted as adequate. To be sufficient in society you must hold a purpose, yet do I have one or am I still searching?

Grudges

Do your best to let go.
I know
it's easier said
as you're unable to stop
holding onto the hate
laced within
your heart.

There's fear you
will become rotten,
like some of the people
who walk this Earth,
but you know
that you want to be better
because you strive for change.

For Victoria

Her face holds strength,
a forest with open arms
as she wakes,
colors filling the sky of her city,
sounds of Rio whispering in the wind,
yet her voice remains soft
like snowfall.

She's shy
but alluring as a gem
when light kisses her skin,
she glows,
her eyes ocean dark,
tell the happiest tales
of her people.

Once her head is carried by the clouds
she feels *apaixonar,*
the stage of falling in love.

Things Left Unsaid

I wanted to tell you

how much I love seeing your eyes

light up the sky

blue storm clouds hidden in your green irises, waiting

like fresh rain in a garden.

Your bright skies never last,

flowers wilting under the sun's touch

rain falling 'til all that's left,

weeds rather than roses

As happy as you were,

tears glazed your eyes.

You hid the pain laced within your body,

smiling as if it was healthy

You

Tender smile and curly hair,
your love beyond comprehension,
like a trance
I can never escape.
I pray your fingertips forever linger
upon my skin,
your voice pulling me in
like a siren near the shoreline,
guiding me home.
Surrounded by flesh and bone,
you engulf me with peace,
assuring me
that *I* can ascend,
rather than fall
into a dream
I never believed
could come true.

Gum

Bittersweet

is how you left me.

Chewed with no remorse,

every time you unwrapped

a piece of me,

I lost a bit of myself,

becoming litter on the floor.

Begged you to spit me out,

yet you kept biting down

knowing I was tired of you

making me tasteless,

molding me into everything you wanted

wadded me up,

stuck me under a table

for someone else to find,

finally letting me go.

Nice Guys

I never liked the nice guys.

The ones
that look like fine wine,
with shaggy hair,
emerald-green eyes.

He looks like paradise
but he's a devil in disguise.

One filled with empty promises,
performed gestures, insecurity
he takes power
lingering beneath my flesh

I should've known
when the roses he gave me
dried into the next sunrise,
leaving nothing but thorns.

There was no love in his heart.

Coronation

Check.

To realize that we were monochrome lovers forged across the stars was beautifully naïve. I wanted to fill your heart with the same desire you had given me, but then you unleashed *your* reality. With no hesitation I was willing to give up the blood in me, so that you could survive, yet you were the villain wielding the blade. A tyrant with charmingly twisted words, luring my heart into a cage that masked manipulation through promises. Although you remained the same, playing emotions like pawns in a chess game, I found my crown.

Checkmate.

Dark Roast

Your love was like fresh coffee brewing strong

and as I drank it

the grounds lingering on my tongue molded

because you became bitter.

Seesaw of The Mind

My mind argues with itself as I lie in bed

thinking back to past regrets and faults,

then looking forward

wondering

Was I good enough?

Am I good enough?

Will I ever be good enough?

I wish I knew who I was,

who I am,

who I'll be next week,

next month,

next year.

Was I ever the best version of myself?

Am I the best version of myself?

Will I ever become the best version of myself?

I'm not quite sure

Cheater

He grew tired of lying awake at night

wondering where he'd gone wrong.

You left him undone,

his heart bleeding out for you

only for it to be burned by salt.

Your careless actions, his destruction.

So, did you have a good time?

Useful

Was I good enough for you?

Bleeding me dry

like a dagger through the heart,

blade pressed into my back.

I was good enough to be bruised by your hands,

only for you to kiss them.

Too dramatic, you said.

I was only good enough when it suited you best,

so, I hope karma fucks you next.

Repeat After Me

I'm enough.

I must let go of that person

I once loved

I'm enough.

I shall no longer be wounded

over the false assurances

offered to me.

I am enough.

Fly

My wings are fractured
but I will soar one day
It'll just take time to mend
from these prior mistakes

even so these black feathers of mine
can kiss the sky,
dance along the clouds,
and glide among the horizon

You can batter me,
discourage me,
claim I'm in over my head.
But I can run and jump
toward my goals in the end.

No longer are my paths blocked,
clearly seeing the other side,
yes, I am a "flightless crow,"
but I refuse to stop flying

Haruichi Furudate, *Haikyuu!!* (Tokyo: Shueisha, October 2012), 5-7.

Thoughts

We live in a society plagued by opinions, separated by law and morals as not every law is just.

Regardless of the togetherness we try to hold onto, the concept of 'world peace' may remain a myth within this reality as everyone carries different perspectives on life

that is what divides us.

If I Had Wings

Sleep hinders as words are whispered and

the owl waits to take flight.

Upon my window, greeting a black sky,

its eyes illuminate the night.

Wind rustles leaves

feathers now spread wide

to roam coolly through the air

freedom as its guide.

The moon sends her dreams

as stars begin to sing

yet my eyes remain open in wonder

of your everything.

Perception

You're a paradox to me.

Your body screams to lay down,

yet you keep working.

Tired, you manage to keep a grin,

eyelids sinking and cheeks flushed as

hickory curls lie on the cotton of your mattress.

Muffled snores escape your plush lips,

the same that whisper tender words,

bringing a restless heart at peace.

You Were Called Courage

Today a sunflower peeked through the field.

Tall against the wind; the sun kissing the gold of their curls.

A soldier of the sun holding a lion's heart,

whose feet linger in the soil,

like grass and its morning dew.

One who has befriended the rain despite its thunder,

shows no fear toward the eyes of disaster.

Chapters

It doesn't matter
if your story begins
like a fairytale
or a nightmare.

As each page passes,
your narrative takes shape,
plot lines becoming more complex,
permitting you to grow.

So continue to laugh,
cry, or scream,
because your dreams are attainable
as long as you believe
in happy endings.

Rediscovery

I want to remind you of a moment

you had never felt so alive,

able to scream

at the top of your lungs

because you felt untouchable,

tears flooding your eyes,

starlight through your fogged-up window.

you cried,

not for sorrow,

but for the freedom in finding yourself,

a voice repressed,

born once more.

Lovesick

Surrender yourself to the heart like clear blue sky,

Let that hue of color

fill your soul with integrity and peace.

May it reveal your deepest desires

and if that heart seeks refuge into your hands,

be the sun so that it may survive.

Dead Poets Society

The sky becomes purple as the cars hum by,

as you remember the trials that continue in your life.

Your love, your loss, your growth.

The film rolls along, you become transfixed

in this conjured parallel, your life mirrored onto a screen,

admiring Robin Williams as you, my friend,

also believe

love is what we stay alive for

Our imperfections painted like Venus on a script.

Whalen 52

Lurking within
this endless abyss,
I remain a whale passing through.
No friend or mate to call my own,
singing and shouting
'til my voice is strained,
yet there's not one song
sung back to me.
I've become a foreign entity
in a strange place called home.
Loneliness clings while in the sea,
though my melody may never reach,
I will keep singing until I'm heard.

ACKNOWLEDGEMENTS

Leo Fernandez	Frank Fernandez
Lourdes Vanegas	Norma Alvarado
Anne E Eck	Laura Sanchez
Kai Grey	Matti Oshin
Emma Andersen	Megan M Fernandez
Elise Fernandez	Alyssa Herrera
Eric Koester	Alison MacDonald
Laura Leon	Ashley Guzman
Ana Leon	Ivy Park
Jeniffer Caceres	Brigitte Keavy
Alanna Bonifazi	Sophie Somerville

Celeste Espinoza	Raeneisha Colson
Aly Jarmon	Makayla Rose Fry
Lacey Goff	Kashai Stanford
Leo Hensley	Nikki French
Caro Hernandez	Jay Cosie
Kelcey Salcedo-Vallejo	Julia Leatham
Kiki Nicolee	Monica Hamada
Denise Domeneck	Marco Leon

Thank you for valuing my dream and supporting me throughout this journey.

I'm forever grateful for your kindness and hope to continue on another path with you.

APPENDIX

Furudate, Haruichi. *Haikyuu!!* vol. 3; Tokyo: Shueisha, October 2012.

Geronimi, Clyde, dir. *Peter Pan*.1953; Burbank, CA: Walt Disney Productions, 1990. DVD.

www.ingramcontent.com/pod-product-compliance
Lightning Source LLC
LaVergne TN
LVHW011846060526
838200LV00054B/4194